TOO MACABRE FOR MONTREAL
Tales Deemed Too Disturbing for MACABRE MONTREAL

MARK LESLIE
SHAYNA KRISHNASAMY

Stark Publishing

STARK

PUBLISHING

TOO MACABRE FOR MONTREAL
Tales Deemed Too Disturbing for MACABRE MONTREAL

MARK LESLIE
SHAYNA KRISHNASAMY

Stark Publishing
Waterloo, ON
www.starkpublishing.ca

Publisher's Note: This is a work of non-fiction that explores darkness and evil acts. The authors of the book do not condone nor endorse such things but have merely collected them together under a theme of events and activities that are considered macabre, and which have occurred in the city of Montreal, Quebec. This is not meant to represent the locale as dark or disturbing. On the contrary, the authors believe that Montreal is a truly magnificent place to live in and visit.

Too Macabre for Montreal
Mark Leslie & Shayna Krishnasamy. -- 1st ed.
eBook ISBN: 978-1-989351-36-9
Trade Paperback ISBN: 978-1-989351-35-2

This one's for the good folks behind Haunted Montreal ghost walk tours, with respect and appreciation.

Table of Contents

Introduction

WHAT IS TOO MACABRE FOR MONTREAL?

W hat is too macabre for Montreal?
Excellent question.
I'm glad that you asked.

This was a topic that came up multiple times during both the writing and the editing process for the October 2018 book **Macabre Montreal:** *Ghostly Tales, Ghastly Events, and Gruesome True Stories* written by Shayna and me.

As we planned out the content of the book, we created an online spreadsheet that we could use for tracking. On it, we denoted the various topics that we wanted to include in the book, some of the sources we knew we'd be able to use for that chapter, as well as a potential title, an estimated word count, and which one of us would take on the writing of that chapter.

Sometimes a story idea would come up, but if it was something that neither one of us was able to properly adapt into a chapter, we left it alone. And every once in a while we would find a tale that we weren't sure would properly fit into a book that had originally been conceived of as a collection of mostly ghost stories concerning the city of Montreal.

Given the alliteration that came with the title, we ended up sourcing a few tales that weren't necessarily supernatural, but were rather, more macabre in terms of their content. Many of the mob stories that we uncovered in our research were within that realm.

It was this combination of ghostly tales and other dark and disturbing events that lead us to the subtitle that was used for the book. The subtitle would help convey to the reader that we took the term "macabre" quite seriously and that we wouldn't just include ghostly tales, but we were also going to share ghastly events and gruesome true stories.

I mean, think about the balance of those three elements.

Ghostly.

Ghastly.

Gruesome.

Yes, that was specifically crafted alliteration in the subtitle. But it also pretty much fit the bill. Certainly, some of the stories shared in the book, including the tale of one of the most famous ghosts of Montreal, Mary Gallagher, the murdered Griffintown prostitute, involves quite grisly and ghastly details. She was, after all, beheaded on June 27, 1879. And, as the legend goes, every seven years she appears on the corner of William and Murray Street in a never-ending quest to look for her head.

The ghosts of the oldest inn in North America, the Auberge Saint-Gabriel, stems from a tragic tale of a young girl and her grandfather who were burned alive because of an act of arson; and that the man ultimately responsible, the son of the old man and the father of the daughter, witnessed the horrific scene; in what some might say is karmic justice for his fraudulent scheme.

Those are just a couple of the tales that cross-over between the ghostly and the gruesome.

But there are still other tales in the book that are dark, disturbing and aren't about ghosts, but are about the darkness, about terrible errors, about evil acts that people are capable of performing on one another.

Such as the 1901 murders of two members of the Redpath family, the unspeakable torturous experiments conducted at McGill University as part of Project MK-Ultra, the accidental beheading by Canada's most famous hangman, the numerous mob-related murders, or the fact that a Montreal student was responsible for the death of famous magician Harry Houdini.

Those, of course, are some of the ghostly and ghastly things that appear in the book **Macabre Montreal**.

But there were some other stories that ended up being cut from the originally submitted manuscript.

One might say they were left to die on the cutting room floor.

Others might say, particularly in the context that we are exploring here, that the "lives" of these chapters were cut short by a cruel hand.

All joking aside, Shayna and I enjoyed the experience of working with the editorial team at Dundurn, the publisher of the book **Macabre Montreal**. But the fact that there were additional tales that didn't make the final cut into the published book, particularly because they were felt to be a little too much, perhaps a little too ugly to include, was also intriguing to us.

I remember joking with Shayna that apparently there were some tales that were deemed "too macabre" for **Macabre Montreal**.

Editorial decisions were made that the tales were too dark, too disturbing, too close to home, and perhaps too controversial, to include in the book.

We reluctantly went with those changes.

But, as we'd spent hours of research on chapters and stories that would never see the light of day in this book, we were also a bit disappointed.

Until now.

We went back to the cutting room floor, to those mangled corpses of tales and snippets of information compiled from the research we had done, and we wanted to offer them up to readers who are able to handle slightly darker, slightly more disturbing content.

Picture us, for a moment, like a pair of twin Doctor Frankensteins – the Hollywood version of the doctor, rather than the literary one – chortling in mad laughter on a stormy night in a hidden lair on the edge of the Mount Royal Cemetery as we picked up those bloodied and abandoned body parts, carefully sewed them together and shouted "They're alive! They're alive!"

Because, after all, the intent of **Macabre Montreal** was to explore the shadows, explore the ghosts, and have a little bit of fun with some of the speculative elements and supernatural tales that make up part of Montreal's rich history.

But the tales you are about to read aren't fun. They aren't spooky.

They're about pure evil.

They're about the nastiness of humanity.

They're about the horrific evil that one human is actually capable of doing to another.

They are, ultimately, tales that were deemed too macabre for Montreal.

- Mark Leslie Lefebvre
October 2020

Watch Me Kill

LUKA MAGNOTTA

L uka Magnotta wasn't always so interesting. He was born Eric Newman in Scarborough, Ontario. He has a sister named Melissa. His parents got divorced and for a time he lived with his grandmother. He was an outcast in high school. None of these details would seem to add up to Magnotta becoming one of the most notorious murderers in Canadian history, and yet, unfortunately, he did. So, how does one go from Eric Newman living in the Toronto suburbs to Luka Magnotta porn star, stripper, and ghastly murderer? Here's how.

Magnotta waited until he was in his twenties to display his unusual side, quickly showing an interest in exhibitionism. Wikipedia lists his early adventures starring in pornographic videos, as well as working as a stripper and an escort. But what's of far more interest is his seeming obsession with getting himself out there in the media. In 2005 he appeared in Toronto's *fab* magazine, which caters to the gay community and often features sexy models. In 2007 he competed in the reality series *COVERguy*, which featured male models competing for a magazine cover feature, a photo shoot, and $1,000 cash. He didn't win.

He also auditioned in 2008 for the reality show *Plastic Makes Perfect* which follows people as they have extreme plastic surgery procedures. His audition tape for this show, detailed in the *Global News* article "'My name is Luka and I'm a cosmetic surgery addict': audition tape," depicts a young man with an alarming and unhealthy need to alter his body to find happiness. In the tape, Magnotta himself lists the procedures he's already had, including a nose job, a procedure to fix the dark circles under his eyes, and two hair transplants to reverse the effects of a receding hairline. His future plans include another hair transplant and muscle implants. The then 22-year-old Magnotta freely states that all he cares about are his looks, that his family doesn't understand these interests and won't speak with him because of them, and that his body is his life. He admits he has these procedures done on his body in order to be accepted.

This clear need to be physically perfect and obvious focus on being seen certainly paint Magnotta as a shallow character, and a narcissist, but don't directly point to the criminal impulses to come. To see that coming we need to make a detour back to 2005 when, as reported on Wikipedia, Magnotta was arrested for impersonating a woman in order to obtain a credit card and using the card to purchase goods worth $10,000. He was convicted of these offences, but sadly didn't see any jail time, getting instead a conditional sentence of nine months and twelve months probation.

Lying about himself, however, wasn't a game Magnotta had any plan to give up. It was around this time that he changed his name from Eric Newman to Luka Rocco Magnotta and began creating various online personas for himself. If you thought Magnotta already sounded kind of weird, trust me, here's where he gets even weirder.

By the time he was arrested in 2012, Magnotta had created 70 Facebook profiles, 20 websites, and hundreds of false online identities. In his *Maclean's* article "Are you Luka Rocco Magnotta's Facebook friend?", Alan Parker explains how Magnotta used his own multiple profiles to create fanciful versions of himself living in exotic places, while the completely fake profiles (some with hundreds of Facebook friends due to a mass-friending strategy) were used to give the impression that Magnotta was more relevant, famous, outrageous, and important than he really was. Some of these fake people would make negative comments about Magnotta, simply to keep his notoriety alive.

Parker also describes Magnotta's documented obsession with connecting himself with infamous murderer Karla Homolka through internet trickery. He went about this strange task by creating fake Facebook profiles using the last names of people connected to Homolka, then friending those fakes with his fake pseudonym profiles, and thirdly sending out friend invites to anyone with the last name Magnotta. In this manner he managed to create a Facebook web of lies in which his name, or his photos, became intertwined with Homolka's, giving the impression that they were in some kind of relationship but were trying to hide it. And just to make sure he really made his point, Magnotta also tried several times to edit Homolka's Wikipedia entry to list himself as her husband.

The weirdest part of this internet deception business is Magnotta's strategy of keeping the buzz about himself alive by denying it. *CTV News* reports that in 2007 he went on a Toronto radio talk show and was interviewed by the *Toronto Sun* about Homolka, and in both instances went on and on about how he was in no way connected with the killer, though he claimed the rumours to the contrary were ruining his life. He said he'd received death threats over the matter. He said someone had stolen his car and killed his dog. The *Toronto Star* reporter, Joe Warmington, later said that even during the interview he'd gotten the feeling Magnotta was just making it all up. Which, of course, he was. But it was the heft of the lies themselves that kept the story alive, making it seem as though *everyone* believed Magnotta was connected with Homolka, when in fact it's possible nobody did.

Lying about himself online certainly seemed to be Magnotta's favourite pastime, that is until he got into murder. He started small.

In 2010, Magnotta uploaded a video called "1 boy 2 kittens" to YouTube. In this video, Magnotta suffocated two of his own cats with a vacuum. In 2011 another video called "Python Christmas" went up in which Magnotta fed a living kitten to a snake. So, there it is, the animal torture police procedurals have taught us all to look for when trying to identify a killer. There's the kernel of what was to come, already popping. But even more significant than the fact that Magnotta was killing his pets, perhaps, was the fact that he was uploading evidence of the deeds to the internet. He didn't just want to kill them. He wanted to be seen killing them. Which brings us finally to the act our killer is best known for, Magnotta's grisly murder of Chinese international student Lin Jun.

As expected, Magnotta went about creating buzz around the murder and the video he planned to make about it before the act was even committed. (Can you say premeditation?) In her article "Christie Blatchford: The chilling online posts that Luka Magnotta jurors were not shown," Blatchford describes one such post that was put online ten days before the murder. Though it isn't clear whether the post is a video or a photo, Magnotta is described as wearing a purple hoodie and holding an icepick as he asks if anyone has seen his own murder video on the deep web, and if he can get a copy. Another post on a psychiatric forum is a great deal longer:

> Firstly, dont worry I am NOT posting graphic details or links to the video, I am just curious as to what would possess somebody to do this sort of crime? There is a video of a guy around aged 20 from San Francisco, he

apparently made real snuff films that depict cannabilisim [sic] and necrophilia along with the murder. I am doing research on this and I would VERY much appreciate any and all the advice and help you could give me. Is he a psychopath or Anti Social or what? I know we dont have a lot of details but based on the crime its self. Thanks in advance.

As this post went up on May 16, nine days before the murder, it's quite obvious now that it had to be Magnotta himself who posted it and purposely included certain false details (his age, and the city of origin). Not surprisingly, Blatchford points out that Magnotta would often shave a few years off his age when posting or speaking about himself.

The buzz created, Magnotta then went about committing his heinous crime. The first step was to film the opening scenes of his murder video in which his victim is still alive. For some reason Magnotta made the decision to film this part of the video with a different man, who has never been identified but must feel incredibly lucky to have survived. Shot on May 18 and 19, the video depicts Magnotta straddling a naked man who is bound at the feet and sleeping. He has a small electric saw in his hand. Though he might have considered it, Magnotta didn't kill this man. Instead he decided to kill Lin Jun.

Nobody knows for certain how the two met. One *Global News* article reports a claim by Magnotta (our serial liar) that he met Lin at a metro station after Lin had replied to his Craigslist ad for sex and bondage. The two men were caught on Magnotta's apartment building's lobby surveillance camera entering together on the evening of May 24. Lin was never seen alive again. The video of the dismemberment of Lin runs eleven minutes long. Magnotta titled it "1 Lunatic 1 Ice Pick" before uploading it to the website Bestgore.com, a shock website for photos and videos of real-life violence. In the video, Magnotta does many heinous and unforgivable things to the body of Lin Jun who is already dead from a slashed throat. Magnotta stabs the victim with an ice pick and a kitchen knife. Magnotta dismembers the victim's body. Magnotta performs acts of necrophilia on the body parts. Magnotta cuts the victim's flesh with a knife and fork. Magnotta allows a dog to gnaw on the body. Wikipedia also reports that in a more extensive video only available to police Magnotta is shown cannibalizing the body.

What happened next shows the level to which Magnotta believed he had risen now that he'd committed and advertised his murderous capabilities. The attention of his internet fans no longer enough to satisfy him, Magnotta began vying for the attention of the highest government officials in the land. After spending the night emptying his apartment of the evidence of his crime, Magnotta went to the post office and mailed some interesting parcels. He mailed his victim's left foot to the Conservative Party of Canada. He tried to send a hand to the Liberal Party, but alas it was intercepted in a mail processing facility. Another hand and foot were sent to schools in Vancouver. And yes, as was his desire, the country took notice.

It wasn't until May 29 that Lin Jun's torso was discovered in a suitcase behind Magnotta's apartment building. He had left it with the trash. The Montreal police stepped in and the pieces of the puzzle began to fit together. The body parts around the country and the torso were matched and later identified as Lin Jun. Papers identifying Magnotta were also found with the torso. Surveillance footage identified Magnotta as the man mailing parcels at the post office. The police had their suspect.

However, Magnotta had already fled the country using the airline ticket he purchased on the night of the murder. He flew to Paris first, but had already vacated his hotel when police arrived there. Then he boarded a bus to Berlin. Magnotta was surely thrilled to know that he was now the subject of an international manhunt, and was being sought by Interpol. In the end it was the Berlin police who nabbed him at an internet cafe. At the moment of his arrest he was reading a news article about himself.

Despite the defense's efforts to get Magnotta off due to his diminished mental health (psychiatrists from both sides diagnosed him with a number of conditions, including schizophrenia, histrionic personality disorder, borderline personality disorder, paraphilia, and narcissistic personality disorder), he was convicted after a twelve-week trial on all counts and sentenced to life in prison.

So, there you have it. The suburban kid from the broken home transformed into the notorious killer. Like it or not, Luka Rocco Magnotta is not a name any of us will soon forget. In the end, he got the attention he wanted, though at the price of a victim mourned by his family, his own freedom, and the hatred of a country. One can't help but wonder if it was worth it or if Magnotta sits in his Quebec jail cell, cooking up more lies, concocting new plans, imagining himself the star of more ghastly videos that have yet to be shot and stories yet to be written.

The Mommy Monster in Suburbia

SERIAL KILLER KARLA HOMOLKA

What if you found out that your mother was an infamous serial killer? Not just a serial murderer, but perhaps the most notorious female child rapist and murderer in the history of Canada.

It seems a horrific premise, an eerie thought-experiment; but it is, sadly, for three Montreal children, a startling and shocking reality. And *Mommy* isn't locked away with a life-long prison sentence. She's right here at home, and also volunteering at their school.

It is an overwhelming truth that, no matter how long ago a terrible tragedy like this happened (more than a quarter century, in this case), the pain, the suffering, and angst are alive and well for the families of the serial killer's victims. But in this particular case, there is a whole new round of potential angst for a new generation of innocent children. This time, the new victims are the ones who were born into an almost unthinkable situation.

In 1993, Paul Bernardo and Karla Homolka, nick-named the "Ken and Barbie Killers" were arrested with charges related to the rape and murder of three teenage girls from Southern Ontario; one of which was Homolka's younger sister, Tammy.

Born in 1970, Homolka grew up in the city of St. Catharines, Ontario which is about a ninety-minute drive from Toronto. She was the eldest of three sisters. While attending Sir Winston Churchill Secondary School, she took a part-time job at a pet shop, and continued to work in veterinary clinics as an assistant after graduating in 1988. This work gave her access to drugs that were later used in the crimes she committed with Paul Bernardo, who she first met in 1987.

Bernardo, who was 23 at the time he met the 17-year-old, proposed to her on Christmas Eve. From all outward appearances, this was an attractive and wholesome couple on route to beginning a productive life of prosperity together. Nobody suspected that the man who had moved into the Homolka home with his fiancé was the *Scarborough Rapist* who had targeted teenage girls and had either raped or attempted to rape as many as twenty-four victims in a five-year period. And nobody suspected the heinous crimes that the two would commit together.

Flashing forward a few years, to December 1992, where Karla Homolka, severely bruised from being beaten on the head, face, and limbs with a flashlight, was removed from the home she shared with her husband Paul and filed charges against him as a battered spouse. During the investigation following this she revealed that not only had Bernardo been abusing her physically and emotionally, but he had also admitted to her his crimes in Scarborough. She also shared what she described as her coerced involvement in the murders of her sister and two other victims, Leslie Mahaffy and Kristen French.

In May of 1993, the government offered Karla Homolka a twelve-year sentence, a plea bargain for her testimony against her husband in the deaths of the three teenagers and his role as the Scarborough Rapist.

But, after a secret stash of videotapes was uncovered, a new layer of horrifying detail was uncovered. Homolka was complicit in those crimes.

Including the vomit-choking death of Karla's sister, Tammy, which had been originally filed as an accidental death. The video-tape evidence, of course, revealed a more heinous story than was originally told to both the police and the Homolka family.

While living in the home of Karla and her parents, Bernardo became obsessed with Karla's youngest sister, Tammy, allegedly peeking in her window and sneaking into her bedroom to masturbate while standing at the side of her bed while the young girl slept. These activities weren't kept secret from his fiancé, Karla. Instead, she assisted him by breaking the blinds in her sister's window to aid in the visibility.

She also used drugs obtained from her employer, secretly sneaking crushed valium into the fifteen-year-old's spaghetti on one occasion, and, on the fateful night of December 23, 1990, adding sleeping pills to the young girl's rum and eggnog drink.

In an act that has been described as a gift of giving her sister's virginity to her fiancé to satisfy his lust and desire, Homolka and Bernardo videotaped the act of the two of them assaulting and raping the fifteen-year-old.

Karla held a cloth soaked in halothane over her sister's nose and mouth, and during the assault, the teenager became sick, choking on her own vomit. The pair proceeded to hide the evidence of the previous evening and that early morning's assault, with the exception of the videotapes, which remained hidden until years later.

In a demonstration of callousness and twisted sensibilities, Homolka complained about the behaviour of her grief-stricken parents in a letter to her friend, and, just a few weeks after her baby sister's abuse and death, she dressed up in her sister's clothes and held a picture of Tammy's face over her own while she and Bernardo had sex.

Only six months after Tammy's death, with both Homolka and Bernardo making plans for their upcoming wedding in Niagara on the Lake, Bernardo kidnapped fourteen-year-old Leslie Mahaffy in Burlington, a town less than an hour's drive from their St. Catherines home.

The couple videotaped the tortured and rape of their victim while listening to music. Homolka explained in a police interview that Bernardo enjoyed sodomizing her while her hands were bound, just as he did to the victim. Except, of course, Karla was not murdered when the act was over.

Homolka testified that Bernardo strangled the girl, while Bernardo claimed the girl died from a lethal dose of Halcion that Homolka fed to her.

During Bernardo's trial, Homolka seemed more shaken by the fact that her fiancé had drunk champagne from a pair of expensive wine flutes than anything related to the kidnapping, torture, and murder of the innocent young girl.

Despite their conflicting testimony of how the girl died, the two worked together to dismember their victim's body and dispose of it encased in concrete blocks that they dumped in nearby Lake Gibson, less than twenty kilometers south of their neighbourhood.

On June 29, 1991, the same day as their Disney-style wedding, Leslie Mahaffy's cement encased body was discovered.

The couple's next hunting, torture, and killing excursion occurred less than a year after their honeymoon. On April 16, 1992 Bernardo and Homolka targeted their next victim, fifteen-year-old Kristen French. Pretending to need assistance, Homolka approached the young girl with a map and the story of being lost. Lured in to help, Bernardo then brandished a knife and forced her into their car.

Again, the couple videotaped the torture, rape, and sodomization of their innocent young victim, with each of them holding the camera while taking terms victimizing her. Homolka shared in an interview with authorities during her "battered victim" statements that she had felt a kinship with French, that the two of them had applied makeup together and gotten to know one another. And, in the cold manner of a sociopath, Homolka was described as being most concerned with fixing her hair after watching the young girl be strangled to death, so that she would look good for the Easter dinner later that day with her parents.

In an interview with police, Homolka described how she convinced her husband of the importance of having an alibi on the same weekend that the St. Catharines girl had gone missing by attending Easter dinner. She also described her uneasiness with going to work after the long weekend knowing that the girl was alive in their home and might possibly escape.

These actions can hardly be interpreted as the acts of an innocent woman who was coerced into rape, torture, and murder; and perhaps more as the signs of a mastermind psychopath with absolutely no regard for another's life and a cold, calculating disposition.

Despite this later videotape evidence as well as testimony from both Homolka and Bernardo about the couple's crimes, the bargain made with the Crown ensured she would only serve a twenty-year sentence and be eligible for parole after only twelve years. It was believed that the lesser evil of this bargain was necessary to secure a full conviction of Paul Bernardo not only for the murders of the three young women, but the rapes of two dozen other women in Scarborough. It was important for Karla Homolka's story to be believed, for the jury to see her as a credible witness. Bernardo's prosecutors continually cast her as a victim, an unwilling accomplice, a woman under the control of her abusive husband.

On May 18, 1993, Karla Homolka was arraigned on two counts of manslaughter. Paul Bernardo was charged with kidnapping, unlawful confinement, aggravated sexual assault, first-degree murder, and dismemberment.

Homolka was originally held in Kingston's Prison for Women, but was moved, in the summer of 1997, to a medium security institution in Joliette, Quebec, which is about eighty kilometers northeast of Montreal.

From all reports, Homolka was a model prisoner and took a correspondence course from Queen's University where she graduated with a Bachelor's degree in Psychology. A three-year relationship that Homolka had with a fellow prisoner named Lynda Veronneau was documented in her French language 2005 book entitled *Dans L'ombre de Karla* (In the Shadow of Karla). In her book, Veronneau wrote about the sex games that involved bondage and stimulated rape which Homolka enjoyed, but also expressed the fact that, despite their catastrophic breakup, she felt Karla was a positive influence on her; that her commitment to her psychology studies inspired her to resume her own studies.

During her two-day release hearing, it was ruled that, upon her release on July 4, 2005, certain restrictions were to be placed upon Homolka, including keeping the police informed of her home address, her work address, and the name of anybody she was living with. She was also required to inform them of any change to her name. She was forbidden to have contact with Bernardo, the families of her victims, or to be with anybody under the age of sixteen.

Within hours of her release, Homolka gave an exclusive interview to SRC, CBC Radio's French language service in order to explain her side of the story. She claimed that she approached French media because they were not as sensational as the country's English media had been, and also expected Quebecers to be more forgiving and lenient towards her.

In a bizarre twist of circumstances, Luke Magnotta (the focus of a different chapter of this book, *Watch Me Kill*), a man convicted of first degree-murder, committing an indignity to a human body, publishing obscene material, criminally harassing Prime Minister Stephen Harper, and mailing obscene and indecent materials, was linked, via a series of different online rumour pools, to Karla Homolka.

The rumors were all, it seems, part of Magnotta's ploy to help create his "bad boy" image, along with what appeared to be an unhealthy obsession with the convicted schoolgirl killer. In a November 3, 2015 article in the *Toronto Sun*, a friend of Magnotta revealed that he regularly discussed Paul Bernardo and Karla Homolka. "He is obsessed with her," the friend said, "and has said he is hopeful she will visit him in prison."

In the spring of 2011, after a lengthy period of research and following leads that included many misdirections, including the afore-mentioned rumours initiated and propagated by Luke Magnotta, investigative journalist

Paula Todd tracked Homolka down. Documented in a June 2012 ebook of approximately fourteen thousand words entitled *Finding Karla: How I Tracked Down an Elusive Serial Killer and Discovered a Mother of Three*, Todd outlined her investigation and a very tense hour spent in Homolka's home in Guadeloupe.

Living under a different name (Leanne Bordelais) and married to Thierry Bordelais, the brother of her Quebec lawyer, Homolka was now the mother of three young children. Todd explained, in great detail, the terse conversation and almost surreal experience of sitting across from one of Canada's most notorious serial killers who, upon all appearances, seemed to be an excellent mother.

Todd describes Homolka as sweet, loving, and motherly, displaying a decidedly maternal disposition with her three children. She expressed that the children seemed clearly accustomed to their mother's gentle attention. "Of all the scenarios I'd prepared for – including physical harm," Todd writes, "–this one takes me by surprise."

And that same seemingly normal motherly behaviour is part of the story revealed not long after the discovery of Homolka having returned to Montreal, living under yet another revised version of the many names she has used over the years: Leanne Teale.

It was discovered that Homolka and her family had been living in Châteauguay since 2014. In a 2016 conversation with *La Presse* reporters who cornered the man when he was returning home from work, Homolka's husband, Thierry Bordelais was quoted as saying "Has anything happened over the past ten years? So why are they worried?" This statement falls in line with the concept of a rehabilitated woman living a new life and being given a second chance. A chance, many would argue, that none of the woman's three young victims were ever given.

In the spring of 2017, the news media learned that Homolka was not only volunteering at the Catholic school that her children were attending, but had also supervised children on a field trip, brought her dog into the school to interact with children, and also attended a class to instruct them about knitting.

Tempers and public controversy were again in the air as the media, the neighbourhood, and the rest of Canada reacted to this news.

Andrew Scheer, leader of the federal opposition in Ottawa made the following statement in the House of Commons: "Our criminal justice system is so broken that one of Canada's most notorious serial killers is now volunteering at a school. As a father, I cannot imagine the horror of listening to my children come home and tell me that they just spent the day with Karla Homolka. It's sick."

"In the name of Jesus, leave her alone," a woman was heard yelling at a crowd of journalists, as reported in a May 31, 2017 *Montreal Gazette* article. "It is written that everyone of us is sinful and we must forgive, because God is a forgiving God. Leave her alone."

"She is a psychopath, and there is no cure for psychopathy," Tim Danson, the lawyer for the Mahaffy and

French families is quoted as saying in that same *Montreal Gazette* article by Jason Magder. "And there could be a sequence of events that could come into play that could trigger her psychopathy."

A Facebook page called *Watching Karla Homolka* that has just under fifteen thousand followers in late 2020 continues to post stories and articles about the infamous serial killer as well as an attempt to post and share her every move.

A Global News article of September 14, 2017 by Amanda Jelowicki entitled "Is Karla Homolka being harassed?" says that some people have questioned whether or not things have gone too far.

David Henry, executive director of L'Association des Services de Rehabilitation Sociales du Quebec is quoted in that article as saying: "If you can't find work if you can't find an apartment, if you can't go to the doctor, if you can't walk in the streets because people stare at you and are afraid of you, basically you cannot do anything in society so it could be a vicious cycle."

Regardless of where one stands on the issue of forgiveness, rehabilitation and retribution, there seems to be one thing most people can agree upon. Homolka's three young children are innocent and unwillingly thrust into both the spotlight and potential harm. Considering how well-known their mother's crimes are and the fact that no matter where they go, they seem to be found, they will likely continue to be prey to the insensitivity of inquiring minds, the media, and perhaps even bullies who attempt to seek retribution for their mother's past crimes.

One of the saddest things to consider in this horrific tragedy is that, on top of the unending pain, angst, and suffering that Karla Homolka's deviance delivered to the Mahaffy and French families and so many of the victims' friends and loved ones, she also made swift victims of her own parents, her own sibling, and her own innocent children.

Three generations of an innocence lost to a monster who walks freely down Montreal streets.

The Head That Would Not Be Silenced

THE TALKING HEAD

Authors Note: This story was included for its humorous and ghostly aspects and is not meant to be taken seriously. The depiction of the Oneidas was taken from source material dating back to 1936 when opinions of indigenous peoples were far less acceptable than they are today. The authors have the utmost respect for the First Nations of Canada and hope no offence is taken by this ridiculous tale.

Throughout history men have killed each other. This is an unavoidable fact. They've killed each other for money, for revenge, for political gain, for sport. But perhaps only once in history has a man been killed for his fine head of hair.

That man is Jean de Saint-Père, a Frenchman, New France colonist, and notary, who on October 25, 1657 was building a house with his father-in-law and their servant in the colony of Ville-Marie (now Montreal). A group of Oneidas, of the Iroquois confederacy, hung out nearby watching the action. There didn't seem to be any hostility between the two groups, as according to the *Montreal Gazette* they shared a meal that day in perfect civility. But as soon as the men went back to their work, things turned murderous. The Oneidas grabbed their firearms and shot all three men dead. The father-in-law, Nicolas Godé, and the servant were both scalped. And poor Saint-Père was completely beheaded so the Oneidas could possess his fine head of hair.

Then, things when from murderous to downright weird. As the warriors were fleeing with their prizes it is reported that Saint-Père's severed head began to speak, or to be more specific, to scold the Oneidas for their crimes. John Robert Colombo writes in *Ghost Stories of Canada* that the head said the following: "You kill us, you inflict endless cruelties on us, you want to annihilate the French, you will not succeed, they will one day be your masters and you will obey them."

It spoke all this in Iroquois, a language Saint-Père did not himself speak.

Not surprisingly, the Oneidas were frightened and alarmed (and one might assume pretty annoyed) by the talking head. Colombo claims they tried everything they could to get rid of it, covering it and burying it and abandoning it, but the voice followed them no matter what they did. Finally they scalped the head like the others and threw the head away, but it was no use. The voice continued, whispering from within the hair itself.

Contemporaries François Dollier de Casson, an original Montreal historian, and the famed Marguerite

Bourgeoys, who founded the Congregation of Notre Dame of Montreal, reported this unlikely story, according to the *Montreal Gazette*. Dollier insisted that he'd heard the story from a reputable source who had heard it from the Oneidas themselves.

Incredible though it might be, the message of this story is clear: Payback was a bitch even in the 17th century.

A Tragedy We Must Not Forget

ÉCOLE POLYTECHNIQUE MASSACRE

Also known as the "Montreal massacre" the École Polytechnique massacre is the deadliest mass shooting in Canadian history. On December 6, 1989 a twenty-five-year-old man armed with a rifle and a hunting knife shot twenty-eight people, killing fourteen women, before killing himself.

We are purposely not mentioning the killer's name because, though this book is about macabre events, he is not the one who should be remembered in this story.

Even more horrifying than the malicious act of the gunman are details related to his attack.

The gunman entered the first classroom, shot into the wall behind Nathalie Provost, one of the surviving eye-witnesses, then yelled at the male students to leave the classroom. He then told the nine women to get into the corner, saying that he was fighting feminism.

"I answered him back," Provost says in a December 2019 *Global News* interview. "that we were not feminists, and if he wants to study at Polytechnique, he can come with us. And then he shot."

"You are all feminists!" he screamed as he fired point blank at all nine of them, killing six.

"It's awful," Provost says, "and you see – I saw – the eyes of a colleague die. And then you know that you will die; that you are the next one. And it takes a second."

He then moved through the school, continuing to target women. By the end, he killed fourteen women and injured ten other women and four men before turning the gun on himself. His suicide note claimed political motives and also laid blame to feminists for ruining his life. Investigators found a list he had created with the names of eminent women on it that had been labelled "feminists to slaughter."

"I have decided to send the feminists, who have always ruined my life, to their Maker," the gun-man wrote in a hastily drawn suicide note. And yet the media avoided recognizing the violence for what it really was.

"There was no reflection on would we cover the violence against women angle," says Shelley Page, a former journalist in the aforementioned December 2019 Global News report, "because that seemed beside the point."

It wasn't until about a decade later that the event was recognized not merely as a mass homicide, but a mass femicide.

Considering the characterization of this attack as an anti-feminist action potentially representative of a larger issue of violence against women, the anniversary of the horrible tragedy has been commemorated since 1991 as the *National Day of Remembrance and Action on Violence Against Women*.

In 2014, on the twenty-fifth anniversary of the massacre, fourteen searchlights representing the fourteen female victims of the massacre were installed on the esplanade of Mount Royal. The light beams turned skyward first appeared shortly after four o'clock, the hour when the attack had started 25 years earlier. That same year, the Order of the White Rose was established, which is a $30,000 national scholarship for female engineering graduate students.

While there is no getting over or making up for the needless loss of life due to this misogynistic act, it should be noted that the incident also led to Canada's adoption of more stringent gun control laws and introduced improvements to the tactical response of police to shootings that were later credited with minimizing casualties at the Dawson College shooting of 2006 in which only one victim was killed.

That, of course, is just the beginning.

Because we have a lot more to do in order to right the societal wrongs that created the atmosphere for such a blatant strike against women.

On April 23, 2018 in Toronto, a man killed ten people by running them over in a van. It was reported as the "deadliest terror attack on Canadian soul since the École Polytechnique massacre" and the man responsible was allegedly motivated by misogyny.

As reported in a December 2018 article in the Huffington Post by Kaitlin Bardswich, while some laws have been put into place, not much has actually changed. In 2017, for example, 84% of Canadian homicide victims killed by either a current or a former intimate partner were women. And in the first eight months of 2018, one hundred women and girls were killed in Canada; primarily by men.

Indigenous women in Canada have it even worse, as they continue to be killed at a rate that is six times higher than the national average.

In a December 2018 Global Newscast, sharing details from the annual ceremony to honor the engineering students who were gunned down twenty-nine years earlier, Catherine Bergeron spoke about the importance of remembering her sister Geneviève as well as something she would like to see.

"What I would like to see in a more general way," she says, "is more tolerance, more *ouverture*, more respect. If we have that in mind, I think everything is possible."

"We must remain engaged in the fight to prevent and address gender-based violence," says Sophie Grégoire Trudeau in that same news report. "We can always do more on this matter. Always. And we have to stand united. This is way beyond the political. It is our human story."

And the story of fourteen students, murdered in cold blood merely because of their sexual identity is the type of story that is told far too often.

As mentioned before, we don't want to waste any space on the name of the man who committed these acts – but, instead, would like to do our small part in honoring the memory of the students whose lives were tragically cut short.

Geneviève Bergeron
Hélène Colgan
Nathalie Croteau
Barbara Daigneault
Anne-Marie Edward
Maud Haviernick
Barbara Klucznik-Widajewicz
Maryse Laganière
Maryse Leclair
Anne-Marie Lemay
Sonia Pelletier
Michèle Richard
Annie St-Arneault
Annie Turcotte

Let us honor them in the best possible way by never losing sight of how much more we have to do to put an end to violence against women.

"I think we realize that women are still very much vulnerable – are still vulnerable in a way that most men aren't," says Francine Pelletier in a December 2019 *Global News* report examining why we remember so passionately and with such commitment, thirty years later. "And we're seeing it now with the 'incel rebellion,' with these men, and the #metoo movement is another indication."

"I said I wasn't feminist, because, for me, thirty-years ago," survivor Nathalie Provost says, "being a feminist meant being involved in a cause, in a group; and I wasn't. I was a student.

"I realize many years after that being a feminist is living in a certain way, and if I define feminist as living in a certain way, and raising my children in a certain way, then I know that I am feminist."

It has taken a long time for the narrative surrounding the Montreal massacre to change. And it is likely to take longer, and a lot more work, for the dark reality of violence against women to be recognized and dealt with.

Montreal's Night of Terror

THE MURRAY-HILL RIOT OF 1969

Authors Note: This story was one Mark had compiled research for but never ended up writing. He was initially attracted to the title of a CBC Television news report that included the words "Montreal's night of terror" when doing research for the book.

Intrigued by the title, he read a number of sources and watched news clips about that evening. But this chapter was cut from the book's line-up before it was even written.

The authors thought, since it captured a dramatic night of violence in Montreal's recent history that it might be worth including in this short collection.

W hat happens when a metropolis has no police and no firemen? Montreal found out last night."

These are the word of David Knapp in a grainy and slightly faded black and white clip from a CBC Special Report entitled "Montreal City in Trouble." The report runs less than six minutes and documents the disturbing events from more than fifty years ago.

The events of that night resulted when the police walked off the job for sixteen hours, following a breakdown in negotiations related to difficult and extreme working conditions. One of the requests was for the annual salary of a police constable to go up from $7,300 to $9,200. This was in recognition that being a police officer in Montreal was far more dangerous than Toronto. Two Montreal officers had been killed in the line of duty the year before in the frequent riots of between French Canadians and English Canadians. Between February 1968 and April 1969, more than forty gangland murders took place in Montreal – this total was more than all of the murders in the previous fifteen years combined. This heightened violence was the result of a younger generation of French-Canadian criminals determined to rise up against and overtake the dominant position and power of the long-running Mafia that had long been dominating the Montreal underworld. Combined with these forty-one gang-related murders, the total number of murders in Montreal in 1968 was seventy-five, resulting in Montreal being referred to as the murder capital of Canada.

Montreal's mayor, Jean Drapeau, had been elected on a promise to clean up the city, the mafia underworld, and to crack-down on corruption. But instead of following through on that promise, he had focused on other large and grandiose projects like Montreal's Expo 67. There was a feeling in the air that the mayor cared more about the privileged upper class and those with power and influence than the poorer working-class citizens.

The tensions continued to mount in such a way that the excusive contract that the Murray-Hill company had with the Dorval airport was seen as symbolic of the type of monopolies that Drapeau allowed to flourish. (Not to mention that the owners of Murray-Hill Limousine service were English-Canadian while the majority of the taxi drivers were French-Canadian – which merely added fuel to the already existing fires within the city.)

During the day, the number of bank robberies doubled, and the city fell into a general state of unease and confusion. But as night fell without police presence, things took a darker turn.

Two hundred Montreal cab drivers belonging to the Mouvement de Libération du Taxi (MLT), who had a history of taking action against the Murray-Hill company (in 1968 they had created blockades, burned vehicles, and even planted a bomb in a Murray-Hill bus that had been diffused before it went off) took advantage of the lack of police presence and congregated in Griffinton to organize a demonstration.

An in-service limousine was attacked, and, while the driver and customers made it out safely, the vehicle was smashed to pieces, rocks and Molotov cocktails were thrown, causing significant damage, and gunfire was exchanged. As the evening progressed, buses were overturned and burned.

After causing considerable damage to Murray-Hill, the demonstrating cabbies, members of separatist political groups and the Popeyes Motorcycle club moved throughout the downtown shopping district, spreading mayhem, damaging shops, hotels, and restaurants, and looting many businesses. A trail of glass and blood that went as far as St Laurent's main district left shops in ruins and vandals took advantage of the riots to ransack the stores and steal merchandise.

The Montreal Gazette reported the following in an article from October 8, 1969.

> Fires, explosions, assaults and a full-pitched gun-battle kept Montrealers huddled indoors as the reign of terror brought the city to the edge of chaos and resulted in the call for the Army help... Hundreds of looters swept through downtown Montreal last night as the city suffered one of the worst outbreaks of lawlessness in its history. Hotels, banks, stores and restaurants around the Ste-Catherine-Peel Street axis had their windows smashed by rock-tossing youths. Thousands of spectators looked on as looters casually picked goods out of store-front windows.

Quebec's Premier, Jean-Jacques Bertrand, stepped in and deployed the army to impose order in the city. By the time the sun again rose on the city, one hundred and eight people had been arrested, thirty people had been injured by gunfire, two people, including a provincial police corporal, were dead, and the damage stood at an estimated two million dollars.

As Montreal was unable to afford a pay increase for the police (the city was still in significant debt from the investment made in projects such as *Expo 67*), the provincial government stepped in and created a new police force for the entire island of Montreal. This ensured that the wealthy suburbs of Montreal would pay for the costs of policing in the city, which resolved the initial issue.

The monopolistic contract that Murray-Hill had with the Montreal airport was also lost. And The Montreal Urban Community (MUC) (Communauté Urbaine de Montréal – CUM) was formed. This was a regional government that covered all municipalities located on the Island of Montreal and the islands of L'Île-Dorval and Île Bizard. It was created in January 1970 and lasted until the end of December 2001; these municipalities were merged into the megacity of Montreal on January 1, 2002.

There have been long been riots in Montreal's past, such as the *Richard Riot* of 1955, or multiple riots related to the Montreal Canadiens winning, and longer ones involving more people and more significant damage, which would include the two day riots in April 1849, for example, that saw a mob invading and burning the Parliament building. The year 2020 alone has already seen plenty of new riots. But this particular riot stands out as one in which the ongoing and historic background of

English-French tension, the working-class versus the upper-class, at a time where the city was virtually defenceless with no police presence.

Which is likely why, to this day, it is still referred to as *Montreal's Night of Terror*.

FURTHER READING

For further reading about macabre Montreal events, including ghostly tales, historic legends, and eerie paranormal and unexplained activity in the city, check out the full book **Macabre Montreal:** *Ghostly Tales, Ghastly Events, and Gruesome True Stories* by Mark Leslie and Shayna Krishnasamy, available in paperback and eBook.

If you are looking for free online reading about Montreal's creepy history, you should definitely check out the Haunted Montreal website at:

https://hauntedmontreal.com/

On the following pages you will also find the sources used in the compilation of these articles for further reading, listening, and viewing.

SOURCES

Sources for Watch Me Kill

Blatchford, Christie. "Christie Blatchford: The chilling online posts that Luka Magnotta jurors were not shown." *National Post,* December 15, 2014. http://nationalpost.com/opinion/christie-blatchford-the-chilling-online-posts-that-luka-magnotta-jurors-didnt-see

Parker, Alan. "Are you Luka Rocco Magnotta's Facebook friend?" *Maclean's,* June 18, 2012. http://www.macleans.ca/politics/are-you-luka-magnottas-facebook-friend/

Pinsky, Amy. "Tracing Luka Magnotta's footsteps: The night Jun Lin is last seen alive."

Global News, December 9, 2014. https://globalnews.ca/news/1708594/tracing-luka-magnottas-footsteps-the-night-jun-lin-is-last-seen-alive/

Unknown. "Internet offers disturbing profile of Luka Rocco Magnotta." *CTV News,* May

31, 2012. https://www.ctvnews.ca/internet-offers-disturbing-profile-of-luka-rocco-magnotta-1.833829

Unknown. "'My name is Luka and I'm a cosmetic surgery addict': audition tape." *Global*

News, June 7, 2012. https://global-news.ca/news/253808/my-name-is-luka-and-im-a-cosmetic-surgery-addict-audition-tape/

Wikipedia. "Luka Magnotta." https://en.wikipedia.org/wiki/Luka_Magnotta

Sources for The Mommy Monster in Suburbia

Blatchford, Christie. "We should remember the horror of Karla Homolka's past." *National Post*, June 2, 2017. Jelowicki, Amanda. "Is Karla Homolka being harassed?" *Global News*, September 14, 2017. https://global-news.ca/news/3745364/is-karla-homolka-being-harassed/

Magder, Jason. "Parents who criticized Karla Homolka say Greaves Academy asked them to Leave." *Montreal Gazette*, May 31, 2017.

Murderpedia. "Karla Leanne Homolka." http://murderpedia.org/female.H/h/homolka-karla.htm

Todd, Paula. *Finding Karla: How I Tracked Down an Elusive Serial Killer and Discovered a*

Mother of Three. Toronto: Canadian Writers Group, 2012. Warmington, Joe. "Magnotta 'obsessed' with Homolka." *Toronto Sun*, November 3, 2015.

Sources for The Head That Would Not Be Silenced:

Colombo, John Robert. *Ghost Stories of Canada.* "The Talking Head." Toronto: Dundurn Press, 2002.

Kalbfleisch, John. "Second Draft: A talking severed head haunts his murderers." *Montreal Gazette,* October 28, 2016. http://montrealgazette.com/ opinion/columnists/second-draft-a-talking-severed-head-haunts-his-murderers

Sources for A Tragedy We Must Not Forget

Wikipedia. "École Polytechnique massacre."

https://en.wikipedia.org/wiki/%C3%89cole_Polytechnique_massacre

Lanthier, Stéphanie. "Polytechnique Tragedy." *The Canadian Encyclopedia.* January 5, 2012 / December 6, 2014. https://www.thecanadianencyclopedia.ca/en/article/polytechnique-tragedy

Bardswich, Kaitlin. "Not Much Has Changed Since The Ecole Polytechnique Massacre." *The Huffington Post.* December 6, 2018. https://www.huffingtonpost.ca/womens-shelters-canada/montreal-massacre-ecole-polytechnique-trudeau_a_23607411/

Laframboise, Kalina. "We Cannot Forget: 14 women killed in École Polytechnique massacre honoured," *Global News*. December 6, 2018. https://global-news.ca/news/4737404/ecole-polytechnique-ceremony-29th-anniversary/

"École Polytechnique massacre: Why we remember 30 years later." *Global News*, December 5, 2019. *YouTube*. https://www.youtube.com/watch?v=xarUlZ28irQ

Sources for Montreal's Night of Terror

Dougherty, Kevin. "1969 police strike left city in chaos." *Montreal Gazette*, October 7, 1999.

Knapp, David. "1969: Montreal's 'Night of Terror'." *CBC News*, October 8, 1969. https://www.cbc.ca/player/play/1707753042

Sancton, Andrew. *Governing the Island of Montreal: Language Differences and Metropolitan Politics*, Berkeley: University of California Press, 1985.

Piper, Grant. "Montreal's Night of Terror: a dark glimpse into a world without law enforcement." *Medium*, June 14, 2020. https://medium.com/history-of-yesterday/montreals-night-of-terror-1e9bd632cdb

ABOUT THE AUTHORS

Mark Leslie is a writer, editor, and all-around book nerd. His first published horror story "Phantom Mitch" received honorable mention in **The Year's Best Fantasy and Horror** and his first non-fiction book of true ghost stories, **Haunted Hamilton** was nominated for the Hamilton Literary Awards. His other non-fiction books about true ghostly and paranormal events include **Spooky Sudbury**, **Tomes of Terror**, **Creepy Capital**, and **Haunted Hospitals**. Mark's fiction – which includes the *Nocturnal Screams* series and the novel **I, Death**, borders on horror, science fiction, and urban fantasy – has been described as a cross between "Twilight Zone" and "Black Mirror" in style. When he is not writing he can often be found haunted bookstores, libraries, and craft breweries.

You can learn more about Mark at www.markleslie.ca

Shayna Krishnasamy loves a good chilling tale in any form, be it whispered around the campfire—or fireplace. She's not actually going camping where there are bugs—or on the big screen—though some report she covers her eyes during the truly gruesome parts (unverified). Shayna has had grisly stories published in *Geist* and *The Fiddlehead*. She is the author of the teen and literary novels **Home**, **Regan** and **The Sickroom**, as well as the new adult romance novels **Put Me Back Together** and **Watch Me Fall Apart** under the pseudonym Lola Rooney. Shayna lives in Montreal with her husband and son, where she jumps when someone knocks on the door too loud (allegedly).

You can learn more about Shayna online at:
www.shaynakrishnasamy.com

OTHER TITLES

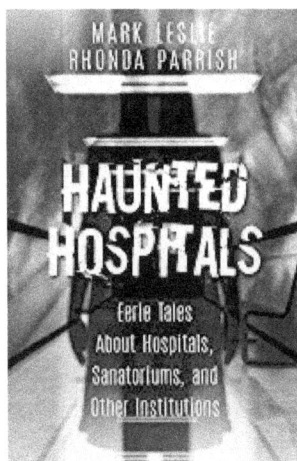

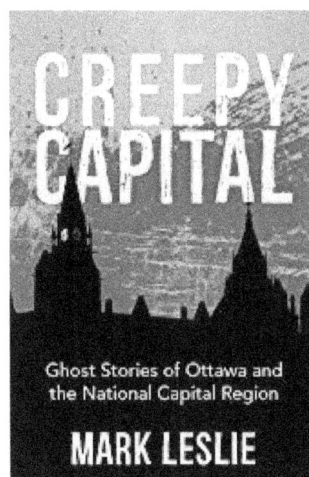

www.ingramcontent.com/pod-product-compliance
Lightning Source LLC
Chambersburg PA
CBHW021222020426

42331CB00003B/427